TRIUMPH OF JOB

TRIUMPH OF JOB

LAURA C. PLEMING

Robert H. Sommer/Publisher
Harrington Park, New Jersey

Published by:
Robert H. Sommer
27 Blauvelt Drive
Harrington Park
New Jersey 07640

**Pleming, Laura C.
Triumph of Job**

Library of Congress Catalog Card Number 78-65452

ISBN 0-933062-00-1

Manufactured in the United States of America

Designed by Barbara Shapokas

Dedicated to the four men in my life:
My dad
My husband
My sons

CONTENTS

	Forward	11
I	My Servant Job	13
II	My Champion Job	19
III	Why Me?	27
IV	You Heretic, Job!	47
V	You Worm, Job!	63
VI	Listen, Job!	75
VII	Arise, Job!	91
VIII	Triumphant Job	99

Forward

Why do the righteous suffer? Philosophers, theologians, doctors, and laymen have offered answers in varied systems of thought and action, in diverse tongues, creeds, and dogmas.

But all the answers ever given have not sufficed to silence all the why's. As long as the world lasts, man will continue to have problems to overcome, and his search will go on for the cause and relief of his pain and frustrations.

Is it trite to suggest that salvation is an individual experience? That perhaps individual man cannot save the world, the nation nor even a cause; but that he can attempt to save himself, and for now that may be enough to support the world?

There was a man in the land of Uz who lost everything: family, wealth, possessions, friends, health, and self-respect. As he wallowed on the ash heap, he cried out against the injustice of fate, and his cry has echoed down the centuries: "Is there any way a man can find surcease from suffering?" "Is there a Power that can be known?" "Why do the righteous suffer?" "Why me?"

Job rose as the Phoenix from his own ash heap. The answers he found were his own answers. His struggle may help and encourage others to leave their ash heaps and find the answers to their questions.

The Book of Job was composed as a drama in poetic form. The Bible translation used here is the classic King James Version with its rhythmical cadence. The verses are arranged as poetry.

11

I   My Servant Job

Job was a patriarch in the land of Uz, a highly respected and honored man. He described his existence: "I washed my steps with butter, and the rock poured me out rivers of oil."

Chap. 29:6

As an esteemed prince, when he came into the city, he was invited to judge at the gate; in fact, he had his own seat, occupied by no one else in his absence. Upon his entrance the elders gave him the respect of rising, and the young men bowed their heads so that their mantles fell over their faces.

Chap. 29

He won approval from his fellow men for his fairness and courage as champion of the

poor and oppressed. His compassion led him to investigate cases of oppression, and often he caused the cruel or unjust to make restitution. His fearlessness and integrity prevented him from being swayed by the prestige of the oppressor. His name was synonymous with righteousness. Thus, as Job discharged his civic duties, he was feared by his enemies and

Chap. 29 honored by the people.

His conduct was above reproach. Knowing the pitfalls of egotism, he consciously avoided vanity, deceit, and pride. Because of his vast wealth, he no doubt had opportunities to deceive his wife and become a pleasure-seeking profligate,

Chap. 31 but such opportunities he steadfastly spurned.

In a day when servants and slaves had no rights as individuals, Job believed the rights of every person were established by the Creator, and he, himself, could not—and would not—annul them. He had the means to assist the poor, and many a widow found food and clothing supplied for herself and her needy children. Orphans found a home in the tent of Job, and no wayfarer ever slept in the cold, or went without food, when he was in the circle

Chap. 31 of Job's possessions.

Job accepted his wealth with dignity, but always acknowledged God (Elohim) as its Source. He felt that as long as he did not offend God, and conducted himself wisely and unselfishly, God would not withdraw His factor

Chap. 1:1,3 from him.

Job did have his sorrows. He worried about his children. His sons no longer lived at home. They gathered together for sumptuous feasts and invited their unmarried sisters to attend among their guests. Job was greatly concerned over these prolonged festivities. He was well aware of the sensuous temptations that enticed one after too much food, wine, music, and exotic dancing by the entertainers. No doubt, he had even alienated his children by what they considered his inflexible attitude. Chap. 1:4,5

At such times Job would sacrifice a series of burnt offerings on behalf of each offspring to atone for any possible breach of behavior. Chap. 1:5

His meticulous conformity to ritual has been suggested as one key to the flaw in his character. Could this be why his sons chose to live away from home? Why were his daughters so anxious to visit their brothers? After all, they were raised in the religion of their father. Was his example so stern and forbidding that his religion held no appeal to his children? And did Job blame their departure upon their weaknesses rather than upon the inflexibility of his own nature?

Perfection can be hard to live with, especially when it is maintained for fear of what might happen if the most minute detail of ritual is overlooked.

Some have claimed that Job's sin was self-righteousness; that he sacrificed to keep evil away. Evil was a powerful reality to Job, and perhaps he feared that God would not protect him if he did not sacrifice continually. If so, Job did not truly know God, the Supreme God. Yet, in spite of all this, Job was the only man on earth that the Lord [Elohim] had for His champion.

18

II   My Champion Job

The poet uses this way of explaining why Job is forsaken: "Now there was a day when the sons of God came to present themselves before the Lord [Elohim], and Satan [the Adversary] came also among them."

Chap. 1:6

Satan of the Chaldean and Persian periods was called the Adversary—the Devil of later centuries. In the earlier periods his only power was to accuse and oppose.

When God demands of the Adversary where he comes from, Satan impudently answers that he has been "going to and fro in

the earth, and from walking up and down in it," looking for a perfect man.

Chap. 1:7

When God reminds him of Job, Satan is highly amused: "Doth Job fear God for nought?"

Chap. 1:9

What does Job lack? Doesn't he have everything? Satan implies that Job worships the Lord only for material wealth.

It had been stated earlier that there was "none like him [Job] in the earth, a perfect and an upright man." Now that assertion is challenged, and the hypothesis is introduced that *Job is the only one pure enough to prove*

Chap. 1:8

*that man can love God without expecting a
material reward!*

And so Job is to be tested.

Shock after shock rocks Job. He has not the
time to recover from one before another is
upon him. In minutes he loses wealth,
possessions, home, income, and family. He is
Chap. 1literally wiped out.

All he has left are his wife and his God.
Could there be a greater time of stress than
this? Men have committed suicide for less. Yet
up to this point, Job's religion sustains him.

To indicate his overwhelming grief, he rends
his garment; but to turn from God never
occurs to him. In fact, he shaves his head to
reaffirm his vow to God, and in an attitude of
abject worship, declares that everything
belongs to God, including himself:

Chap. 1:21,22

> *Naked came I out of my mother's
>   womb,
> And naked shall I return thither:
> The Lord gave, and the Lord hath
>   taken away;
> Blessed be the name of the Lord.*
>
> *In all this Job sinned not,
> Nor charged God foolishly.*

Thus Job passes the first test.

The poet-dramatist returns to the Court of
the Lord, and the Adversary again challenges
God. For just a moment the mask is removed
to reveal the purpose of Satan: *Who is to be
God*—good, or evil? Elohim, or Satan? And Job

22   *MY CHAMPION JOB*

becomes God's champion. The stakes are high.
The prize is Job's life. Chap. 2:4-6

Severe as the first trial was, Job has yet to
suffer another. The first had destroyed his
whole substance; the second will threaten to
destroy his very soul. It will devour his will
to live.

With this, the poet-dramatist begins to
answer the question, "Why do the righteous
suffer?" It may have been unjust for Job to
suffer. Was it any more just for Jesus?

The disease that mortified Job's body was Chap. 2:7
called boils, loathsome sores, leprosy.
Whatever the malady, he was covered with
open, running ulcerations as repellent as they
were painful. In such an unsightly condition,
the only place he was allowed to stay was on
the city dump or ash heap.

The rubbish of his day was the rotting
debris of the city — dung ashes,
maggot-infested carcasses, foul smelling
garbage. Here jackals slink and snarl at howling
Orient dogs. Here city urchins and village
idiots hurl stones at the unfortunate sufferer
and shout with glee at every wince of pain.
The once-respected prince, now an outcast,
takes broken pieces of pottery to scrape the
pus and corruption that his carbuncles exude, Chap. 30:1,8-12
looking forward to the daily visit of his wife as
his only comfort.

As she watches him grow steadily worse, she
can no longer stand his anguish. Death by a
curse is better than a slowly dying life, and she
wildly suggests the theological method of

commiting suicide. In her grief and hysterical misery, she may have convinced herself that Job deserves his fate:

Chap. 2:9 *Dost thou still retain thine integrity? Curse God, and die.*

There is no mention of his wife after this, so now all Job has is his God. And what a God He is! A God Job does not know or understand, a capricious God: loving one moment, destructive the next, capable of good and evil, using man as a pawn to bless or torment as He chooses.

Gossip is a juicy plum. Word spread rapidly about Job's misfortunes, especially as the doctrine of divine retribution was accepted by everyone: prosperity was the outward sign of inward piety, and its loss the obvious sign of hidden sin. With such degradation as Job suffered, conjectures ran wild, gradually becoming assumed fact.

Chap. 2:11 When Job's three friends hear the news, with attendant grim details, they resolve to meet and hasten to Job's side. They hope to obtain a confession of guilt that will absolve Job's soul from destruction. They are good men and good friends, their motive pure and loving. How could they dream their counsel would bring only greater anguish to their old friend?

Eliphaz, "God is gold," is the oldest. He is a Temanite, a desert dweller. The pedantry of his religious philosophy reflects the barren land in which he lives.

Bildad, "son of strife," is a Shuhite, a pit dweller. His dogmatic conformity to traditional theology reveals no hope to one in the depths of despair.

Zophar, "twitter (like a bird)," is a Naamathite, an easy liver. The line of least resistance appeals to him. Whoever has the strongest argument will have his support. His applied orthodoxy glosses the surface nicely.

These three come to comfort Job. When they see their old friend, they are appalled. When last they saw him, he was at the zenith of his strength. Now he is emanciated, weak, diseased, unrecognizable. Their dismay is so overwhelming, that they immediately perform the funeral rites of mourning for him. Chap. 2:12

Poor Job! So in need of comfort, yet his friends' rejection of his appearance, shown by their bereavement ritual, only emphasizes the hopelessness of his deterioration and situation.

For seven days and nights they give him the comfort of their presence without uttering a word. This is indeed a great gift. Chap. 2:13

How long, *how long*, has Job yearned for some expression of kindness! Until now he has been the object of the town's loathing. The children of the vulgar torment him with mocking derision. They spit on him. They throw stones and clods of dirt.

His reputation has been torn to shreds. Not enough evil can be said about him. The very ones whom he championed deride him. Chap. 30

His three friends come and give him the comfort of their silent companionship in his miserable state.

26

III Why Me?

At last Job speaks. From the abyss of his Chap. 3:1-10
physical despair and mental distress, he cries out
his hopelessness. Feeling sure his friends will
understand, he curses the day in which he was born.

He laments he did not die at birth. With
increasing frenzy (oh, the comfort of speech is
so great!), he moans for death. In death there
is a peace to the body regardless of one's
former station in life. Why can't the wish for
death bring death about? Chap. 3:11-19

> *Wherefore is light given to him* Chap. 3:20-22
> *That is in misery,*
> *And life unto the bitter in soul;*
> *Which long for death,*
> *But it cometh not;*
> *And dig for it more than*
> *For hid treasures;*
> *Which rejoice exceedingly,*
> *And are glad,*
> *When they can find the grave?*

Then *he* confides to his friends:

> *For the thing which I greatly feared*
> *Is come upon me,*
> *And that which I was afraid of*
> *Is come unto me.*
> *I was not in safety,*
> *Neither had I rest,*
> *Neither was I quiet;*
> *Yet trouble came.* Chap. 3:25,26

Job had maintained the hope most people
nurture: for security, comfort, and peace in old
age. Yet he had feared that somehow, in spite
of his wealth, evil, as a reality, would strip him

of all he possessed. Now it had happened. In period of stress, he turns to his friends for solace.

His friends glance at each other. Maybe it was too much to hope, they agree, that Job would admit to them his very apparent transgression; they will have to persuade him diplomatically to reveal his offense.

What will follow have been called the three debates. They are the contentions between Job's former religious beliefs, represented by his friends, and Job's current impatience at his friends' obdurate bigotry.

His friends argue for an admission of guilt. To them, it is the only hope for Job's salvation. He replies that their arguments are based on false premises. For him, there must be better answers.

So, gently, the oldest speaks first. Eliphaz reminds Job that he had comforted many in their deep distresses; that his words had given solace and guidance.

Chap. 4:3-5

> *But now it is come upon thee, and*
> *thou faintest;*
> *It toucheth thee, and thou art*
> *troubled.*

Cautiously, he reminds Job that it is the righteous who are saved, and the wicked who suffer from their sins:

Chap. 4:8

> *Even as I have seen,*
> *They that plow iniquity,*
> *And sow wickedness,*
> *Reap the same.*

To clinch it, he tells of a dream, a vision so
mysterious, so supernatural, that his bones felt
like gelatin and his hair stood on end. The
apparition declared:

Chap. 4:14,15

> *Shall mortal man be more just*   Chap. 4:17-19
> > *than God?*
> *Shall a man be more pure than his Maker?*
> > *Behold, he put no trust in his servants;*
> > *And his angels he charged with folly:*
> *How much less in them that dwell in*
> > *houses of clay,*
> > *Whose foundation is in the dust,*
> > *Which are crushed before the moth?*

Eliphaz's only comfort is the doctrine of
original sin, in which man has no hope ever of
knowing purity or forgiveness. To Eliphaz, man
is unclean, while God is an impersonal Judge.
No one can hope to escape:

> *Yet man is born unto trouble,*   Chap. 5:7
> *As the sparks fly upward.*

For Job, this misunderstood doctrine no
longer affords comfort; he is already crushed
under a load almost impossible to bear. What
comfort in the thought that the sins of his
forebears must be borne by him, that God is
the Great Castigator?

Yet it is to this that Eliphaz murmurs piously:

> *I would seek unto God,*   Chap. 5:8
> *And unto God would I commit my cause:*

Eliphaz has already emphasized God's indifference to the concerns of man; he then reverses his position and declares the great things that God does for His creation.

Because the works of God are mighty and unsearchable, Eliphaz urges Job to be patient:

Chap. 5:17
> *Behold, happy is the man*
> *Whom God correcteth:*
> *Therefore despise not thou*
> *The chastening of the Almighty:*

It's all for your own good, Job, he says, no longer diplomatic, probing for Job's confession:

Chap. 5:27
> *Lo this, we have searched it, so it is;*
> *Hear it, and know thou it for thy*
> *good.*

Before Job had experienced his great travail, his convictions were very much the same as those of Eliphaz. Those convictions were no longer enough.

Throughout the disputes that follow, the three friends never change their positions. More and more openly they accuse Job of great guilt. But Job emerges a different person. He tries at first to persuade his friends that they are wrong, that man can suffer without having committed a sin.

Restive under the burden of belief that man cannot question his fate, Job becomes bolder and bolder in his quest for spiritual knowledge, and the breach between him and his friends

grows greater and greater. The first tired belief
he discards is the tenet of man's innate impurity.

When Job answers Eliphaz, he is yearning for
understanding, so he tries to show his friends
the weight of his anguish. He sees that his
friends have not understood his first outburst,
poured out of a tormented heart, and he
knows it is because they have not had his
experience:

> *Doth the wild ass bray when*   Chap. 6:5
>   *he hath grass?*
> *Or loweth the ox over his fodder?*

Of course not. In their prosperity and
health, it is not possible for his friends to
understand.

Less wildly, Job asks again for death, but he
adds a declaration of his innocence. His friends
have wronged him by implying he has sinned,
and as for patience:

> *What is my strength,*   Chap. 6:11,12
>   *That I should hope?*
> *And what is mine end,*
>   *That I should prolong my life?*
> *Is my strength the strength of stones?*
> *Or is my flesh of brass?*

He reproaches them for their lack of pity:

> *To him that is afflicted*   Chap. 6:14
>   *Pity should be shewed from his friend;*

> *But [even if] he forsaketh*
> *The fear of the Almighty.*

Job then compares his friends to a desert brook that appears and disappears without apparent reason. Once a caravan will pass by, and the brook will be flowing where it can be seen; the next time the thirsty travelers come searching for relief from the heat, the brook will have disappeared.

So have you been to me, he tells his friends. When he first saw them, they were as a drink of water to a parched throat; but their mercy has disappeared. All Job wants is the true sympathy of intelligent understanding, and Chap. 6:15-21 even this is withheld.

Chap. 6:22,23
> *Did I say, Bring unto me?*
> *Or, Give a reward for me of your*
> *substance?*
> *Or, Deliver me from the enemy's*
> *hand?*
> *Or, Redeem me from the hand of the*
> *mighty?*

His outburst of bitter disappointment is so great, that his friends resentfully prepare to depart. But disapproving companionship is better than none at all, and he urgently appeals to their pity:

Chap. 6:29
> *Return, I pray you,*
> *Let it not be iniquity [Let there be*
> *no injustice];*
> *Yea, return again,*

> *My righteousness is in it [My cause*
> *is righteous].*

And then he adds:

> *When I lie down, I say,* Chap. 7:4-6
> *When shall I arise, and the night be*
> *gone?*
> *And I am full of tossings to and fro*
> *Unto the dawning of the day.*
> *My flesh is clothed with worms*
> *And clods of dust;*
> *My skin is broken,*
> *And become loathsome.*
> *My days are swifter than a weaver's*
> *shuttle,*
> *And are spent without hope.*

In his great depression, Job sees no hope of
resurrection; there is no hope of life after death:

> *As the cloud is consumed* Chap. 7:9
> *And vanisheth away:*
> *So he that goeth down to the grave*
> *Shall come up no more.*

He reaffirms his right to be impatient, to
complain about his anguish.

Then he commits another unpardonable
offense—he appeals to Deity as an equal! He
does not admit that he has sinned, but even *if*
he had, how could he be a threat to God?

> *Why hast Thou set me as a mark* Chap. 7:20b,21
> *against Thee,*
> *So that I am a burden to myself?*

> *And why dost Thou not pardon my*
> *transgression,*
> *And take away mine iniquity?*

This is too much for Bildad, the dogmatic conformist. In a burst of indignation, he asserts that Job can't convince *him* that he has done nothing wrong; Job is nothing but a windbag!

Chap. 8:2

In his blind anger, Bildad thrusts at Job in the place where it wounds most: Job's children have sinned against the Lord, and they have been punished for their own transgressions—isn't *that* enough proof to Job of divine retribution?

Chap. 8:4

Scornfully, Bildad continues:

Chap. 8:5,6

> *If thou wouldest seek unto God*
> *betimes [diligently],*
> *And make thy supplication to the*
> *Almighty;*
> *If thou wert pure and upright;*
> *Surely now He would awake for thee, ...*

Bildad appeals to Job's instruction in his religion. The tradition of the fathers supports Bildad's contention. There is no place for the questioner and seeker. Besides, there is the law of cause and effect, and the effect of Job's transgressions is very evident to Bildad:

Chap. 8:8-10

Chap. 8:11

> *Can the rush grow up without mire?*
> *Can the flag grow without water?*

He accuses Job of being a hypocrite. The only way Job can hope for divine salvation is to change his attitude:

> *Behold, God will not cast away a* Chap. 8:20
> *perfect man,*
> *Neither will He help the evil doers:*

Thoughtfully, Job answers:

> *I know it is so of a truth:* Chap. 9:2a

For this had also been Job's conviction. He had
accepted it in blind submission. Now he
questions:

> *But how should man be just* Chap. 9:2b
> *with God?*

Job has been urged to become pure and
upright. But how does one begin? How does
one get to know God? His magnitude is
unsearchable, and He is a Spirit:

> *Lo, He goeth by me,* Chap. 9:11
> *And I see Him not:*
> *He passeth on also,*
> *But I perceive Him not.*

In spite of his temerity, Job realizes he cannot
relate himself to God, nor could he justify
himself had he the chance. He would feel
overwhelmed:

> *If I had called,* Chap. 9:16
> *And He had answered me;*
> *Yet would I not believe that*
> *He had hearkened unto my voice.*

Job is convinced that God is responsible for his condition. But given the chance, how will he vindicate himself?

Chap. 9:20,21

If I justify myself,
*   Mine own mouth shall*
*   condemn me:*
If I say, I am perfect,
*   It shall also prove me perverse.*
Though I were perfect,
*   Yet would I not know my soul:*

At this low point in his mental wrestlings, he gets his first glimmer that *evil is not of God*!

Chap. 9:24c

If not,
*   Where and who is he?*

If God does not send these evils, Job questions, WHO does? (And Satan, who has been listening apprehensively, trembles in the shadows.)

Job has mused on the possibility of talking with God, and the idea has captured his fancy. Back and forth his thoughts fly as he carries on an imaginary conversation. Yet he reminds himself:

Chap. 9:32

For He is not a man, as I am,
*   That I should answer Him,*
And we should come together in
*   judgment.*

In desiring justice and conciliation, he deplores the absence of a mediator:

> *Neither is there any daysman*   Chap. 9:33
>   *betwixt us,*
> *That might lay his hand upon us both.*

If there were one, Job asserts that he would be
bold enough to speak. No longer does he fear
death, so the Awfulness of God would not
intimidate him. If only he *could* speak to God,
then:

> *I will say unto God, Do not condemn me;*   Chap. 10:2
> *Shew me wherefore Thou contendest*
>   *with me.*

In reverie, Job daringly challenges his
Maker as to His purpose in creating man. Did
God fashion man to be capable of evil? Does
God incite man to misdeeds, then punish him
for the thoughts He has given him?

> *Is it good unto Thee that Thou*   Chap. 10:3
>   *shouldest oppress,*
> *That Thou shouldest despise the work*
>   *of Thine hands,*
> *And shine upon the counsel of the*
>   *wicked?*

It is God that has made man, he asserts. It
is HE that created the body, the spirit, the
soul, and man belongs exclusively to God. But
for that reason, should God find satisfaction in
punishing man unjustly?

Job's friends have accomplished one thing:
Job is beginning to question his old beliefs,
which no longer satisfy him. *Does* God bring evil
to His creation? Job begins to doubt that He does.

> *Thou hast granted me life and favour,*
> *And Thy visitation hath preserved my*
>   *spirit.*

But the thread of this hope is too fragile, and it breaks in Job's despair. It must be that there is no divine justice; the loss of his former convictions is added to his debility.

> *Are not my days few?*
> *Cease then, and let me alone,*
> *That I may take comfort a little,*
> *Before I go,*
>   *Whence I shall not return,*
> *Even to the land of darkness*
>   *And the shadow of death;*

In this land where death is eternal, there is no light or hope. Thus, Job's first attempt to reason with God ends in a sob of hopelessness.

Zophar, the last of the three friends to speak in this first debate, angrily brushes aside any thought of Job's sincerity.

Job is a rank heretic! His words are boasting and mockery! How can such a man be justified? How can a man who is a groveling sinner dare make the statements and demands that Job has made?

> *For thou hast said, My doctrine is pure,*
> *And I am clean in Thine eyes.*

In asking to speak to God, Job is not misguided—he is damned! Yet for an instant

Zophar wishes that God would speak, and
show Job what a miserable worm he is!

> *But oh that God would speak,*   Chap. 11:5,6
> *And open His lips against these;...*
> *Know therefore that God exacteth of thee*
> *Less than thine iniquity deserveth.*

Job has related God's omnipotence to himself;
Zophar declares that this is heresy, and Job
deserves all that has happened to him. No one
can find God:

> *Canst thou by searching find out God?*   Chap. 11:7-9
> *Canst thou find out the Almighty unto*
>   *perfection?*
>   *It is as high as heaven; What canst thou do?*
>   *Deeper than hell; What canst thou know?*
> *The measure thereof is longer than*
>   *the earth,*
> *And broader than the sea.*

Certainly that should put Job's questionings in
their place. What *right* has he to ask? No
answer will be granted to him. Zophar refers
to Job when he says:

> *For vain man would be wise,*   Chap. 11:12
> *Though man be born like a wild ass's*
>   *colt.*

Then Zophar recalls that he has come to help
save Job. He concludes his denunciations with
an appeal that Job admit his guilt, repent, pray
for forgiveness, and amend his ways. Then he
will have favor in the eyes of God. However,

Zophar hastens to warn sternly:

Chap. 11:20
> *But the eyes of the wicked shall fail,*
> *And they shall not escape,*
> *And their hope shall be as the giving up*
> *Of the ghost.*

The bleating of such platitudes by his friends rouses Job's anger, and he sarcastically answers:

Chap. 12:2
> *No doubt but ye are the people,*
> *And wisdom shall die with you.*

They have told Job nothing he does not already know:

Chap. 12:3
> *But I have understanding as well*
> *   as you;*
> *I am not inferior to you:*
> *Yea, who knoweth not such things*
> *   as these?*

These are the trite truisms that Job had preached and practiced his whole life, but he can't convince his friends that these are not adequate in a time of stress.

The almightiness of God is not to be disputed. Job knows that His perfection and power are continual; these are His attributes. But WHERE IS HE?

Job's complacent attitude before his ruin has given way to that of an impatient seeker for Truth. He desires to find God, to know what Truth is. Release from pain and suffering is of small consequence in comparison with the all-important question: What is God, and where can He be found?

Chap. 12:7-25

Surely I would speak to the Almighty,
And I desire to reason with God.

Job considers his friends to have misrepresented the situation. He is not afraid to come into God's presence. He has no fear regarding his past conduct:

Though He slay me, yet will I trust in
Him:
But I will maintain mine own ways
before Him.
He also shall be my salvation:
For an hypocrite shall not come before
Him.
Hear diligently my speech,
And my declaration with your ears.
Behold now, I have ordered my cause;
I know that I shall be justified.

Chap. 13:15-18

Job now knows which questions he would ask of God. Although no answers have been forthcoming, he has begun to formulate the why's, and he muses upon the brevity of life:

Man that is born of a woman
Is of few days, and full of trouble.
He cometh forth like a flower,
*   And is cut down:*
He fleeth also as a shadow,
*   And continueth not.*

Chap. 14:1,2

Job wonders if perhaps God *does* know the ways of a man, even though it has been said of Him that He is so far above men that He takes no notice of them:

Chap. 14:3

> *And dost Thou open thine eyes upon*
>   *such an one,*
> *And bringest me into judgment*
>   *with Thee?*

Man's life is so short; is there no hope for him? But look at the tree:

Chap. 14:7-9

> *For there is hope of a tree,*
> *If it be cut down,*
>   *That it will sprout again,*
> *And that the tender branch thereof*
>   *Will not cease.*
> *Though the root thereof wax old in*
>   *the earth,*
> *And the stock thereof die in the ground;*
> *Yet through the scent of water it will*
> *And bring forth boughs like a plant.*

Is man less than a tree?

Chap. 14:10

> *But man dieth, and wasteth away:*
> *Yea, man giveth up the ghost,*
> *And where is he?*

Job earlier contended that there was no hope for life after death. Now comes his question: *Is* there hope for resurrection?

Chap. 14:14   If a man die, *shall* he live again?

In forming the question, Job shows that he can believe that there is life after death. As his

spirit struggles upward, his bodily pain drags
him downward; and he ends his speech in
agony, as he protests how misfortune may
strike one:

> And thou destroyest the hope of man.
> Thou prevailest for ever against him,
>   And he passeth:
> Thou changest his countenance,
>   And sendest him away.
> His sons come to honour,
>   And he knoweth it not;
> And they are brought low,
>   But he perceiveth it not of them.
> But his flesh upon him shall
>   have pain,
> And his soul within him shall mourn.

Chap. 14:19c-22

During this first round of debate, Job's
friends have maintained that he has sinned and
his misfortunes are the result, but they have
remained hopeful that he would repent and
confess. He has crushed this hope with the
persistent conviction that he has not sinned
and that God's justice is not merciful.

At the beginning of this polemic, his
despair is so overwhelming, that all he can
desire is oblivion. By the end of the first round
of argument, however, he has made three
significant strides forward: he has doubted for
a moment that it is God who visits evil upon
His creation; he has begun to desire Truth
more than surcease from pain; he has begun to
wonder if it is life, and not death, that is
eternal.

The second debate begins...

IV You Heretic, Job!

Gentle Eliphaz is outraged. An ethical formalist
who believes that goodness and reward come
through the exact performance of duty, he
sees in Job's rebellion the breakdown of
religious ideals.

Such talk as Job's is as devastating as the
east wind and shows great ignorance. Even
worse, Job would do away with the very   Chap. 15:2
foundations of religion! He would talk to God
as an equal! Such blasphemy would completely
obliterate devotion and worship:

> *Yea, thou castest off fear,*   Chap. 15:4
> *And restrainest prayer before God.*

What would happen to religion, Eliphaz
demands, if man became equal with God? If
man could even talk with God?

If man no longer fears God, how can man
worship and obey Him? Eliphaz's following
scornful questions apparently fall upon fertile
ground in Job's deliberations, since later there
is evidence that Job searches deeply for
the answers:

> *Art thou the first man that was born?*   Chap. 15:7,8
> *Or wast thou made before the hills?*
> *Hast thou heard the secret of God?*
> *And dost thou restrain wisdom to thyself?*

Does Job think he has a monopoly on
knowledge? Contemptuously, Eliphaz asks:

> *What knowest thou, that we know not?*   Chap. 15:9
> *What understandest thou, which is not in us?*

He reminds Job of the prolonged age of his comforters, since length of days is evidence of unquestioned wisdom and righteousness. *They* have subscribed to the doctrine of man's impurity before God:

Chap. 15:14-16

What is man, that he should be clean?
And he which is born of a woman,
 That he should be righteous?
Behold, He putteth no trust in His
 saints;
Yea, the heavens are not clean in His
 sight.
How much more abominable and
 filthy is man,
Which drinketh iniquity like water?

Why, Job, your desire to talk and reason with God is spiritual pollution! In the pride of his advanced years, Eliphaz boasts:

Chap. 15:17

I will shew thee, hear me;
And that which I have seen I will declare;

Then he paints a picture of all the adversity that overtakes the unrighteous. When the punished evil-doer remonstrates, he will know that he has received his just penalty:

Chap. 15:20-33

Chap. 15:34,35

For the congregation of hypocrites
 Shall be desolate,
And fire shall consume the tabernacles
 Of bribery.
They conceive mischief,
And bring forth vanity,
And their belly prepareth deceit.

There is no pity in Eliphaz's denunciation. Stern, formalistic views have no compassion for the sufferer accused of breaking with traditional duties.

Then the cry bursts from Job's lips:

> *Miserable comforters are ye all!* Chap. 16:2

Is this how you comfort others? Job assures them that he, too, could purse his lips, shake his head, and mutter, "Tsk, tsk" were he in their position, and they in his. He flares out at them:

> *But I would strengthen you with my* Chap. 16:4
> *   mouth,*
> *And the moving of my lips should*
> *   assuage*
> *   Your grief.*

But this is not his fate. He grieves for the loss of his friends' good will. In the face of all his other tribulations, to have his friends denounce him is bitter gall:

> *They have gaped upon me with their* Chap. 16:10
> *   mouth;*
> *They have smitten me upon the cheek*
> *   reproachfully;*
> *They have gathered themselves together*
> *   against me.*

In the depths of this heartbreak, he is unknowingly on the verge of a great truth. It is not God who devastates. Rather:

Chap. 16:9c   *Mine enemy [the adversary]*
                          sharpeneth his eyes
                          Upon me.

Job clings to his spiritual integrity, and asserts his innocence:

Chap. 16:16,17   *My face is foul with weeping,*
                          And on my eyelids is the shadow of
                               death;
                          Not for any injustice in mine hands:
                          Also my prayer is pure.

Even though his friends scorn his declaration, Job's conviction stands:

Chap. 16:19-21   *Also now, behold, my witness is in*
                               heaven,
                          And my record is on high.
                          My friends scorn me:
                          But mine eyes poureth out tears unto
                               God.
                          O that one might plead for a man
                               with God,
                          As a man pleadeth for his neighbour!

These very declarations appear to make Job stronger, because he asks where hope can be found if he admits to corruption and accusations that are untrue:

Chap. 17:13-15   *If I wait,*
                          [If] The grave is mine house:
                          [If] I have made my bed in the
                               darkness.
                          [If] I have said to corruption,

> *Though art my father:*
> *To the worm,*
> > *Thou art my mother,*
> > *And my sister.*
> *And where is now my hope?*
> *... who shall see it?*

Bildad now reacts and mockingly assures Job
that anyone as insignificant as he is, does not
matter one whit in the scheme of the
Almighty. He accuses Job of talking too much:

> *How long will it be ere ye make an end*   Chap. 18:2
> *Of words?*

> *Shall the earth be forsaken for thee?*   Chap. 18:4
> *And shall the rock be removed out of*
> > *his place?*

Bildad puts into words those
self-condemnations that tear at a destitute,
forsaken mortal, doubly significant because
voiced with the authority of dogmatic
tradition. He rants on, avowing that the
conscience of an evil man will condemn him
even if he doesn't admit his wrongs:

> *Terrors shall make him afraid on*   Chap. 18:11,12
> > *every side,*
> > *And shall drive him to his feet.*
> *His strength shall be hunger-bitten,*
> > *And destruction shall be ready at*
> > *his side.*

Bildad describes the calamities that come
upon the evil man. It is no coincidence that

these calamities are the very ones that have befallen Job. Bitingly, Bildad again reminds Job of the loss of his sons, and of the curse that he shall have no descendant.

Chap. 18:17-19

His remembrance shall perish from the earth,
And he shall have no name in the street.
He shall be driven from light into darkness,
And chased out of the world.
He shall neither have son nor nephew Among his people,
Nor any remaining in his dwellings.

Bildad pompously ends his denunciation of Job's attitude:

Chap. 18:21

Surely such are the dwellings of the wicked,
And this is the place of him that knoweth not God.

Bildad's harangue had begun with "How long...," and Job, under pressure of indignant outrage, counters these reproaches with:

Chap. 19:2,3

How long *will ye vex my soul,*
And break me in pieces with words?
These ten times have ye reproached me:

To Job, his prosperous friends, knowing him and his good deeds, have dealt unjustly in their accusations. They are like overscrupulous magistrates dealing out unmerciful decrees on no evidence other than their own prejudices, magnifying themselves because they have not suffered such distress.

> *And be it indeed that I have erred,*
> *Mine error remaineth with myself.*
> *If indeed ye will magnify yourselves*
> *against me,*
> *And plead against me my reproach:*

Chap. 19:4,5

Again, Job mourns that there is no intercessor:

> *Behold, I cry out of wrong,*
> *But I am not heard:*
> *I cry aloud,*
> *But there is no judgment.*

Chap. 19:7

In self-abasement, Job tries to arouse the sympathy of his friends by enumerating the adversities that have cursed him. There is nowhere for him to turn; his kinsfolk, family, and servants, regard him as a stranger.

Chap. 19:13-17

> *All my inward friends abhorred me:*
> *And they whom I loved are turned*
> *against me.*

Chap. 19:19

And more, even his flesh has forsaken his bones. Seeing that no sympathy is forthcoming, he wails for pity:

> *Have pity upon me, have pity upon me,*
> *O ye my friends;*
> *For the hand of God hath touched me.*
> *Why do ye persecute me As God,*
> *And are not satisfied with my flesh?*

Chap. 19:21,22

How profound the degradation is, when a once-proud man must beg for pity. And how much deeper the wound must be, when that pity is stonily withheld. Forsaken by friends, slandered and abused by them, where can he turn?

Job has not transgressed, and he knows it. In this moment of utter devastation, he turns to the purity of his own soul. And from that inner purity, he receives his answer!

Chap. 19:25,26

> *For I know that MY REDEEMER*
> > *LIVETH,*
> *And that He shall stand at the latter*
> > *day*
> > *Upon the earth:*
> *And though after my skin*
> > *Worms destroy this body,*
> *Yet in my flesh shall I see God!*

In an upsurge of positive conviction, Job passionately continues:

Chap. 19:27

> *Whom I shall see for myself,*
> *And mine eyes shall behold, and not*
> > *another;*

The emotion is so overwhelming, that he nearly faints at his own outburst, but has strength enough to turn aside the vilification of his former friends and warn:

Chap. 19:28,29

> *But ye should say,*
> > *Why persecute we him,*
> *Seeing the root of the matter*
> > *Is found in me?*

Be ye afraid of the sword:
For wrath bringeth the punishments of
the sword,
That ye may know there is a
judgment.

This is just too much for Zophar. His complacency has been shaken and his beliefs threatened. He interrupts Job with a tirade that lasts for 57 lines, the only equal of which might be Jonathan Edwards' famous sermon, Chap. 20:1-29 "Sinners in the Hands of an Angry God." James Strahan, in *The Book of Job*, comments upon the "indecent enthusiasm" of this whole speech.

Carried away by hyperbole, Zophar gives vent to self-righteousness in his heartless discourse:

> *Knowest thou not this of old,*   Chap. 20:4,5
> *Since man was placed upon earth,*
> *That the triumphing of the wicked is*
> *short,*
> *And the joy of the hypocrite but for a*
> *moment?*

In the next 47 lines, he savors the consequences of wickedness with such exquisite delight, that it seems possible he himself might have indulged in these very sins—were he not checked by fear of the consequences. His malice completely spent, Zophar finishes:

> *This is the portion of a wicked man*   Chap. 20:29
> *from God,*

> *And the heritage appointed unto him*
> *by God.*

Job may suspect his old friend of secret yearnings, and with some of the old twinkle in his eye, he prepares his friends for his next speech, warning that he intends to shock them:

Chap. 21:5,6

> *Mark me, and be astonished,*
> *And lay your hand upon*
> *your mouth.*
> *Even when I remember I am afraid,*
> *And trembling taketh hold on*
> *my flesh.*

What is this horror he is about to reveal? His friends have been harping on the evil that overcomes the wicked. They are positively enjoying their vilifications, savoring them like sweet morsels. So Job asks:

Chap. 21:7,8

> *Wherefore do the wicked live,*
> *Become old, yea, are mighty in power?*
> *Their seed is established in their sight*
> *With them,*
> *And their offspring before their eyes.*

What about it, my friends? How do you explain this? Job describes the prosperity, happiness and influence of reputedly wicked men who are accepted in good society, have little trouble with the law, and whose children have the best and are happy. Such men dishonor God; yet at their death, they are not treated differently than the most pious of men:

> *They spend their days in wealth,*
> *And in a moment go down to the*
> *grave.*
> *Therefore they say unto God, Depart*
> *from us;*
> *For we desire not the knowledge of*
> *Thy ways.*
> *What is the Almighty, that we should*
> *serve Him?*
> *And what profit should we have,*
> *If we pray unto Him?*

Disdainfully, Eliphaz answers that *he* wouldn't know; *he* doesn't associate with the wicked:

> *The counsel of the wicked is far*
> *from me!**

Job insists upon an answer:

> *How oft is the candle of the wicked*
> *put out!*
> *And how oft cometh their*
> *destruction upon them!*
> *[That] God distributeth sorrows in His*
> *anger.*
> *[That] They are as stubble before the*
> *wind,*

Bildad retreats into the traditional cant:

---

*Verses 16, 19, 22 have been recognized by some scholars as protests interpolated into this speech of Job. See *Job* Anchor Bible, Peake's *Commentary* and Moulton's *Modern Reader's Bible*. It is from the arrangement of Chapter 21 in *The Modern Reader's Bible* that the assignment of the speeches in vss 16, 19, 22 was taken.

God is only concerned with His own.

Chap. 21:19   *God layeth up His inquity for His children:*

Comforting doctrine; "Whom the Lord
Prov. 3:12 loveth, He correcteth." But lets the children of
disobedience go scot-free. Even if Bildad's
reaction could be interpreted as the effect of
heredity, that the sins of the wicked are visited
upon their innocent children, where is the
justice in such doctrine?

Zophar stays upon an exalted but safe plan of
human knowledge:

Chap. 21:22   *Shall any teach God knowledge?*
Seeing He judgeth those that are high.

In other words: "We can't know everything,
Job!" But Job has not finished his discourse
upon the evidence of unequal treatment
between the evil and the good. What
difference does it make, he asks, whether a
man is good or wicked? His end is the same:

Chap. 21:23,25,26   *One dieth in his full strength,*
Being wholly at ease and quiet.

And another dieth in the bitterness of
    his soul,
And never eateth with pleasure.
They shall lie down alike in the dust,
And the worms shall cover them.

Bitterly, he points out that the wicked have
big, sumptuous funerals:

> *Yet shall he be brought to the grave,*
> *And shall remain in the tomb.*
> *The clods of the valley shall be sweet*
> *unto him,*
> *And every man shall draw after him,*
> *As there are innumerable before him.*

Accusingly, he flays his friends with the accusation that they are not able to answer his questions:

> *How then comfort ye me in vain,*
> *Seeing in your answers there*
> *remaineth Falsehood?*

During this second debate, the position of the three friends still has not changed. However, their accusations are no longer thinly veiled, but open and direct. Job's uncompromising attitude has estranged them, and they feel justified in their hostility toward him.

In losing the good will of his former friends, Job tastes the bitterness of being forsaken, and in a state of utter desolation, he turns to the only remaining hope—his own inner purity. In this moment of self-knowledge, he knows that the answer to his prayers will come; and he will understand God.

He has impatiently brushed aside the doctrine that human goodness insures immunity from sickness and evil. Despite his friends' platitudes, he has seen the innocent suffer and the unrighteous prosper.

At the beginning of the third debate, Job the seeker, the impatient one, still searches for the answers to these inequities ...

V   You Worm, Job!

In a burst of wrathful indignation, Eliphaz rebukes Job. He sarcastically asks him if he thinks he can tell God anything.

Chap. 22:2,3

Can a man be profitable unto God,
As he that is wise may be profitable
Unto himself?
Is it any pleasure to the Almighty, that
Thou art righteous?
Or is it gain to Him, that thou makest
Thy ways perfect?

Then in a fit of outrage, he accuses Job of actually committing all the crimes that have been maliciously rumored of him:

> *Is not thy wickedness great?*   Chap. 22:5-7
> *And thine iniquities infinite?*
> > *For thou hast taken a pledge from*
> > *thy brother for nought,*
> > *And stripped the naked of their*
> > *clothing.*
> > *Thou hast not given water to the*
> > *weary to drink,*
> > *And thou hast withholden bread*
> > *from the hungry.*

> *Thou hast sent widows away empty,*   Chap. 22:9
> *And the arms of the fatherless have*
> *been broken.*

These are the serious charges: to have taken
a pledge for nothing, to have refused water and
food to the thirsty and hungry, to have sold
the orphan into slavery. Serious, indeed.

Using a point of agreement—the belief in
divine transcendence—Eliphaz tricks Job into
concurrence:

> *Is not God in the height of heaven?*   Chap. 22:12
> *And behold the height of the stars,*
> > *How high they are!*

Job has never denied God's omnipotence.
Eliphaz uses this to rend Job, misquoting him
at that!

> *And thou sayest, How doth God know?*   Chap. 22:13,14
> *Can he judge through the dark cloud?*
> *Thick clouds are a covering to Him,*
> > *That He seeth not;*
> *And He walketh in the circuit of heaven.*

Chap. 21:14,15   When Job had used these words, he had been deploring the prosperity of the wicked and their renunciation of God. Eliphaz appears to assume deliberately that the speech was actually Job's own repudiation of God.

Ironically, Eliphaz exhorts Job to embrace the very experience for which Job has been yearning since the beginning of the debates:

Chap. 22:21,22
*Acquaint now thyself with Him, and
    be at peace:
Thereby good shall come unto thee.
Receive, I pray thee, the law from His
    mouth,
And lay up His words in thine heart.*

Charging Job with transgressing ethical standards, Eliphaz urges him to renounce moral turpitude:

Chap. 22:26-28
*For then shalt thou have thy delight in
    the Almighty,
And shalt lift up thy face unto God.
Thou shalt make thy prayer unto Him,
    And He shall hear thee,
    And thou shalt pay thy vows.
Thou shalt also decree a thing,
And it shall be established unto thee:
And the light shall shine upon thy ways.*

To Job, the burden of hopelessness again seems more than he can bear. To be accused of unethical deeds, when he has been the model of righteousness, is a greater blow than bodily pain.

> *Even today is my complaint bitter:*   Chap. 23:2
> *My stroke is heavier than my*
>   *groaning.*

Eliphaz has entreated him to return to God,
but Job yearns to know where God is:

> *Oh that I knew where I might find Him!*   Chap. 23:3,4
> *That I might come even to His seat!*
> *I would order my cause before Him,*
> *And fill my mouth with arguments.*

     In this supreme moment of facing God, Job
knows that all his questions will be answered.
Nor will God treat him as a non-entity, as his
friends have implied. Instead, understanding
and reason will be bestowed on him:

> *I would know the words which He*   Chap. 23:5,6
>   *would answer me,*
> *And understand what He would say*
>   *unto me.*
> *Will He plead against me with His*
>   *great power?*
> *No; but He would put strength in me.*

     Eliphaz has said, "Return unto the
Almighty," but *where* is He?

> *Behold, I go forward, but He is not there;*   Chap. 23:8-10
> *And backward, but I cannot perceive Him;*
> *On the left hand, where He doth work,*
>   *But I cannot behold Him:*
> *He hideth Himself on the right hand,*
>   *That I cannot see Him:*
> *But he knoweth the way that I take:*

Even though his friends have not answered his questions, and have misconstrued his remarks, Job is spiritually awakened enough through their questioning, that answers begin to come to him.

Earlier, Job had declared that God was far from him and paid no attention to him; now he asserts that God knows where he is and what he does. Earlier, he said that God was unknowable, now:

Chap. 23:13,14

> *But He is in one mind, and who can*
> *turn Him?*
> *And what His soul desireth, even that*
> *He doeth.*
> *For He performeth the thing*
> *That is appointed for me:*
> *And many such things*
> *Are with Him.*

Bildad, the pedantic conformist, going beyond his comprehension, straddles Job's questions in rebuttal of Eliphaz, by reiterating the impurity of man. Coupling this with a declaration of God's transcendence and omnipotence, he then insists that Omnipresent Being cannot be found!

Chap. 25:2-6

> *Dominion and fear are with him,*
> *He maketh peace in His high places.*
> *Is there any number of His armies?*
> *And upon whom doth not His light*
> *with arise?*
> *How then can man be*
> *justified God?*

Or how can he be clean that is born of
*   a woman?*
Behold even to the moon, and it
*   shineth not;*
Yea, the stars are not pure in His sight.
How much less man, that is a worm?
And the son of man, which is a worm?

Bildad has succeeded in weaving a web so
complicated that there seems to be no way of
escaping it. This doctrine of inescapable
despair Job denounces:

How hast thou helped him that is   Chap. 26:2
*   without power?*
How savest thou the arm that hath
*   no strength?*

Since "the Spirit of God" is the breath in his
nostrils, Job knows that God's omnipresence *is*
discernible, and he refutes the charge of man's
impurity, because he knows that his own
moral being, his spiritual integrity, is intact:

Till I die I will not remove mine   Chap. 27:5,6
*   integrity from me.*
My righteousness I hold fast,
*   and will not let it go:*
My heart shall not reproach me
*   So long as I live.*

   Zophar's harsh answers to Job's declaration
portray Job's present suffering and loss as
proofs of his wickedness; and Zophar ends
with the pleasant thought that both God and
man will deride Job in the time of his extremity.

Chap. 27:22,23

For God shall cast upon him, and
*   not spare:*
He would fain flee out of His hand.
Men shall clap their hands at him,
And shall hiss him out of his place.

Job has long since given up hope of solace
from his friends. His thoughtful meditation
(Chapter 28) on how to seek out understanding
shows that he has hardly heard Zophar's
last harangue.

Job reasons: man has discovered how to mine
gold and silver. Through cleverness, he has
learned to sink a shaft for a mine, where he
finds precious stones and brings hidden
treasures to light. But what of a truer search:

Chap. 28:12

But where shall wisdom be found?
And where is the place
*   of understanding?*

Wisdom and understanding are the true
treasures. They cannot be found in earthy
vaults or watery caverns. No one can purchase
them—even with all the wealth in the world:

Chap. 28:18,19

The price of wisdom is above rubies.
The topaz of Ethiopia shall not equal it,
Neither shall it be valued with pure gold.

Chap. 28:21 Can wisdom and understanding be found if "it
is hid from the eyes of all living"? Does death
or destruction hold the mysteries of life? Job
reassures himself:

> *God understandeth the way thereof,*   Chap. 28:23
> *And He knoweth the place thereof.*

How can Job be so sure of God's omnipresence? Because, he reasons, God is the Creator of the heaven, the earth, the rain, the seas—all the mysteries of creation. Only an all-knowing, all-wise God could create such wondrous complexity!

As Job's thought turns away from himself and toward the allness of God, he is able to answer his own enigmatic question:

> *Behold, the fear of the Lord, that*   Chap. 28:28
> *is WISDOM;*
> *And to depart from evil*
> *is UNDERSTANDING.*

Before his trials on the ash heap, he had believed in a God that embodied both good and evil. Now, at this moment of revelation, he denies that evil is a quality of God.

Unfortunately, he does not sustain this exalted plane of thought for long. He looks back into the past and loses his high revelation. As he laments over the loss of his family, his prestige, his influence for good, his leadership, he becomes more and more overcome with grief.

Unable to dam the flood of self-pity, he   Chap. 29:1 to 30:14
compares his present condition to his former position. The contempt of the very people he had helped, the derision of those he had disciplined, the taunts of the children, are bitter maledictions.

Continuing his laments, his physical body becomes so weak and miserable, that he feels his end is near:

Chap. 30:16,17

> *And now my soul is poured out*
> *upon me:*
> *The days of affliction have taken hold*
> *upon me.*
> *My bones are pierced in me in the*
> *night season:*
> *And my sinews take no rest.*

Regardless of the cost, which could be his life, Job stands before the moment of death and asserts his integrity, making his "oath of clearance." In his soul-searching, he examines all the hypothetical immoral and unethical acts he could be accused of, so that he may face his Creator with a clear conscience and a pure heart.

Chap. 31:1-40 In his oath of clearance, which requires his last ounce of strength, Job declares that: he had avoided vanity and deceit; he had not accepted a bribe; he had not committed adultery; he was not unjust to his servants; he had not oppressed the poor; he had not mistreated a widow or an orphan; he had not rejoiced in the destruction of his enemy; he had not refused a stranger lodging; he had not taken anything that was not his!

To enforce his oath, he demands that swift judgment be visited upon him on the spot, if his declarations are not true.

As he sinks down exhausted from his passionate plea of innocence, his friends refuse to speak to him. To them, he is "righteous in his own eyes," and they cannot condone such self-glorification.

Men love to exhort their less fortunate fellows to change their ways. When their advice is taken, the advisors enjoy the satisfaction of having their own superior understanding corroborated. But when their advice is spurned, the advisors withdraw in cold, angry silence, and dare the suppliant to advance himself.

In this third cycle of verbal exchange, Job's supposed comforters openly condemn him and pronounce him guilty of a gamut of misdeeds. Job had hoped, no doubt, for sympathy and comfort from his friends; but the more he maintains his principles, the further he alienates his companions.

At the moment when he thinks he is on the brink of death, he has no one to turn to. This yawning emptiness is supplanted by a hope that brightens from a glimmer to a promise, turning into faith in a Being whose omnipotence is good, and *only* good. As he realizes the purity of his own being, he perceives the Omnipotent Being as pure.

In order to know the Omnipotent Being fully, Job thinks he will have to die first. He recognizes that man expresses knowledge when he departs from evil, which is no part of Omnipotent Good. Job thinks this is as exalted a revelation as he can understand.

All earthly hope has vanished. There is no place to go, nor anyone to turn to, for understanding, solace, or peace.

"The words of Job are ended"!   Chap. 31:40

74

VI   Listen, Job!

A new member of the cast is introduced: Elihu, "My God is He," the son of Barachel, "God is blessed." Elihu is of the family of Ram (Aram), "exaltation," a descendent of Buz, the brother of Uz.

Elihu is a young man: enthusiastic, sensitive, eager, warm-hearted. These are qualities that Eliphaz, Bildad, and Zophar have long ago lost. Elihu has been listening to the exchange between Job and his companions, and his heart has swelled with indignation toward them all.

Job's need is great, yet his associates have magnified themselves by condemning him;

they have failed to give him a reply. But Elihu
is indignant with Job, too. Job has not been
able to find as righteous an action in God as he
has found in himself.   Chap. 32:2,3

Many of Elihu's affirmations sound similar
to the arguments of the older men, but the
statements are radically different because the
older companions only mouth them with no
sense of fervent conviction.

Elihu speaks with the warmth of awakened
vision, and breathes into dead words the living
fire of truth. This vibrant inspiration is the
mediator for which Job has passionately yearned.

As Elihu speaks, the three companions
withdraw themselves and haughtily refuse to
listen to such juvenile ramblings. Job does not
answer Elihu because he has exhausted himself
with his oath of clearance. But he does listen,
and the effect of Elihu's declarations causes him
to forget himself and ponder Deity's omnipresence.

Respectfully, Elihu begins:

> *I am young,*   Chap. 32:6,7
> *And ye are very old;*
> *Wherefore I was afraid,*
> *And durst not shew you*
> *mine opinion.*
> *I said, Days should speak,*
> *And multitude of years should*
> *teach wisdom.*

Listening to the previous lengthy conversations,
Elihu has discovered that abundance of years
does not always provide great wisdom. To him,
they all have distorted views of God.

Divine inspiration is not the possession of a few, but is given liberally to all men:

Chap. 32:8,9

> *But there is a spirit in man:*
> *And the inspiration of the Almighty*
> *Giveth them understanding.*
> *Great men are not always wise:*
> *Neither do the aged understand judgment.*

Having made such a bold statement, he falters. No one speaks to him, either to encourage or discourage. The silence is so frightening, that he wonders if it would be better not to continue:

Chap. 32:15b, 16

> *They left off speaking.*
> *When I had waited,*
> *(For they spake not, but stood still,*
> *And answered no more;)*

Quelling his self-doubt, he courageously decides to go on and try to help. At least, he won't feel guilty for holding back and not sharing an answer.

Chap. 32:17

> *I said, I will answer also my part,*
> *I also will shew mine opinion.*

Moreover, his enthusiasm will not let him stay silent. Besides having youth, he is sincere. He will not allow the importance of a man's position to dissuade him from speaking, nor will he flatter to add weight to his words. For Elihu, everyone is important in God's eyes.

God is very close to Elihu; in fact, Elihu declares that God is his life:

> *The Spirit of God hath made me,*
> *And the breath of the Almighty hath*
> *given me life.*

Does that sound reasonable to you, Job? If
it does, then you regard God as I do. What is
true of me, is true of you. If God is my life, He
is yours also:

> *Behold, I am toward God as you are.*
> [Revised Standard Version]

Chap. 33:6

Job has lamented that even though he is
clean and innocent, God has judged him
wrongly. Elihu quotes Job's words, and quotes
correctly. He does not imply that Job has
deliberately lied; instead, he emphasizes that
man must reconcile himself to God and seek
His ways—and not expect God to reconcile
Himself to man.

Job had groaned that God does not reveal
Himself to man; Elihu points out that God *does*
speak, but man does not recognize Him:

> *For God speaketh once,*
> *Yea twice, yet man perceiveth it not.*
> *In a dream, in a vision of the night,*
> *When deep sleep falleth upon men,*
> *In slumberings upon the bed;*

Chap. 33:14,15

In those divine moments God instructs man,
often causing him to change his purpose, and
thus protects him:

> *He keepeth back his soul from the pit,*
> *And his life from perishing by the sword.*

Chap. 33:18

Chap. 33:19-22   Elihu describes those periods of illness when food is abhorrent, and the body is emaciated with sickness. The sufferer alternately desires and fears death. At this desperate time, Elihu assures Job that there is help. An interpreter, an understanding being, reveals to man his purity and becomes his deliverer.

Chap. 33:23-26

If there be a messenger with him,
An interpreter, one among a thousand,
To show unto man his uprightness:
Then he is gracious unto him,
And saith,
    Deliver him from going down
        to the pit:
    I have found a ransom.
His flesh shall be fresher than a child's:
He shall return to the days
    of his youth:
He shall pray unto God,
    And He will be favourable unto him:
And he shall see His face with joy:
For He will render unto man his
    righteousness.

When the substratum of purity is revealed, the ransom is paid for man's life. In this revelation of ecstatic joy, man prays to God, and divine mercy cancels the debt.

Gen. 32:30   As Jacob saw the angel on Peniel and declared, "I have seen God face to face, and my life is preserved," so the sufferer will also behold the goodness of God and be restored. In the glow of health, he joyfully reports to his fellow man how he has been healed. Elihu reminds Job that this does not happen only once in man's lifetime, but many times.

> *Lo, all these things worketh God*   Chap. 33:29,30a
>   *Oftentimes with man,*
> *To bring back his soul from the pit,*

Elihu has soared in inspiration while sharing all this with Job, and he turns to him for some response. There appears to be none. Job, exhausted, is unable to answer.

Undaunted, Elihu turns to the three companions. They have censured Job unmercifully:

> *For Job hath said, I am righteous:*   Chap. 34:5,6
> *And God hath taken away my*
>   *judgment.*
> *Should I lie against my right?*
> *My wound is incurable without*
>   *transgression.*

Elihu asks the three friends where they can find a man like Job who will take the scorning of his advisors with such humility, and drink it up like water? They denounced Job because he said that to worship God for material profit is ungodly.

> *For he hath said,*   Chap. 34:9
> *It profiteth a man nothing*
> *That he should delight himself with God.*

[Yet this is exactly what God had told Satan: that man can love God without expecting a material reward!]

The three patriarchs interpret Job's wretched condition as the outward evidence of inward sin. It is God who has visited this destruction upon him as a punishment. Elihu declares this doctrine to be irreverent and blasphemous:

Chap. 34:10
Therefore hearken unto me,
Ye men of understanding:
Far be it from God,
That He should do wickedness;
And from the Almighty,
That He should commit iniquity.

Chap. 34:12
Yea, surely God will not do wickedly,
Neither will the Almighty pervert
judgment.

God is not the author of evil. If He were, and meted out punishment to all mankind as they deserve:

Chap. 34:15
All flesh shall perish together,
And man shall turn again unto dust.

Even in temporal affairs, a man does not judge a king or a noble, and declare his acts vile. Nor would the governed allow a ruler to inflict injustice upon them without a revolt. If this is so in temporal affairs, then is it not so in divine? The omnipresent Being, the Creator, the Just, is not to be regarded as existing on the same plane as man, nor with the same passions. By the same reasoning, the Creator has an interest in His creation. The three aged patriarchs have said that God knows nothing of

man's affairs, nor does He care. The patriarchs
are wrong:

> *For His eyes are upon the ways of man,*   Chap. 34:21
> *And He seeth all his goings.*

At the proper time, the wickedness of the wicked
shall be destroyed, whether it is man or nation:

> *That the hypocrite reign not,*   Chap. 34:30
> *Lest the people be ensnared.*

How many, Elihu asks, are willing, like Job, to
be instructed out of the errors that have
caused their sufferings? No. They ask for relief
from pain, but not at the cost of repentance
and reformation:

> *Surely it is meet to be said unto God,*   Chap. 34:31,32
> *I have borne chastisement,*
> *I will not offend any more:*
> *That which I see not teach Thou me:*
> *If I have done iniquity,*
> *I will do no more.*

Suffering mortals want relief in their own
way, and are not willing to conform to the
Divine Will. This has not been Job's sin. He has
been rebellious, resentful. And in such an
attitude, reconciliation with God is impossible.
Because Job has not known the reasons for his
testing, he has sullenly declared that he is
more righteous than God.

> *Job hath spoken without knowledge,*   Chap. 34:35
> *And his words were without wisdom.*

But is Job's attitude worse than the attitude of his friends, that one must give obedience to God, so that one will receive material benefits?

Chap. 35:2,3

Thinkest thou this to be right,
That thou saidst,
My righteousness is more than
God's?
For thou saidst,
What advantage will it be unto
thee?
And,
What profit shall I have,
If I be cleansed from my skin?

The sins of the friends are greater than the sin of Job.

Elihu exhorts Job to lift his thought to contemplate infinity:

Chap. 35:5

Look unto the heavens, and see;
And behold the clouds which are
higher than thou.

Elihu's reason for pointing to the heavens is different than that of Eliphaz when he said:

Chap. 22:12

Is not God in the height of heaven?
And behold the height of the stars,
How high they are!

or Zophar, when he said:

Chap. 11:8

It is as high as heaven;
What canst thou do?

> *Deeper than hell;*
> *What canst thou know?*

or Bildad:

> *He hath compassed the waters*   Chap. 26:10,11
>   *with bounds,*
> *Until the day and night come to an end.*
> *The pillars of heaven tremble*
> *And are astonished at his reproof.*

The three friends were emphasizing the great gulf between God and man in their speeches; Elihu is stressing the infinite concern and compassion of God. The attitude of "What can He do for me?" must be changed to "What can I do to glorify Him?" Man must seek God to know His infinite design and plan:

> *If thou sinnest,*   Chap. 35:6,7
>   *What doest thou against Him?*
> *Or if thy transgressions be multiplied,*
>   *What doest thou unto Him?*
> *If thou be righteous,*
>   *What givest thou Him?*
> *Or what receiveth He of thine hand?*

Many cry out because of their oppressions, but how many think to shout their gratitude for past benefactions? Or even for present gifts? Elihu continues:

> *But none saith, Where is God my Maker,*   Chap. 35:10,11
>   *Who giveth songs in the night;*
> *Who teacheth us more than the*
>   *beasts of the earth,*

> *And maketh us wiser than the fowls
> of heaven?*

All the loveliness of the earth expresses
God. How superficial you are when you say
that He cannot be found.

Chap. 35:13,14a
> *Surely God will not hear vanity,*
> *Neither will the Almighty regard it.*
> *Although thou sayest thou shalt not*
> *see Him, . . .*

There is a divine plan:

Chap. 36:4b,5
> *He that is perfect in knowledge is*
> *with thee.*
> *Behold, God is mighty, and despiseth*
> *not any:*
> *He is mighty in strength and wisdom.*

In this plan there may appear to be injustice,
but the divine purpose will become apparent.
In a time of great affliction, to desire death is
as wrong as to commit iniquity. Death does
not promote the divine plan:

Chap. 36:20,21
> *Desire not the night,*
> *When people are cut off in their*
> *place.*
> *Take heed, regard not iniquity:*
> *For this hast thou chosen rather than*
> *affliction.*

In the throes of affliction, one learns to crave
and grasp truths not sought before. The
omnipotent Mind of God becomes man's

teacher, and man learns that he magnifies and expresses God:

> *Behold, God exalteth by His power:*   Chap. 36:22-24
> *Who teacheth like Him?*
> *Who hath enjoined Him His way?*
> *Or who can say,*
>   *Thou hast wrought iniquity?*
>
> *Remember that* thou magnify His work,
> *Which men behold.*

God's inscrutable, eternal nature is impossible to know:

> *Behold, God is great, and we know*   Chap. 36:26
>   *Him not,*
> *Neither can the number of His years*
>   *be searched out.*

From the allusions in the remainder of Elihu's oration, we see a storm that has been brewing begin to break. Elihu uses the falling rain, the thunder and lightning, the wind, and the increasing intensity of the storm to illustrate God's government and power in His universe.

Man cannot comprehend the majesty and power of God's creation, yet He governs it all in perfect harmony:

> *Hear attentively the noise of His voice,*   Chap. 37:2-5
> *And the sound that goeth out of His*
>   *mouth.*
> *He directeth it under the whole heaven,*
> *And His lightning unto the ends of the*
>   *earth.*

> *After it a voice roareth:*
> *He thundereth with the voice of His*
>   *excellency;...*
> *God thundereth marvellously with His*
>   *voice;*
> *Great things doeth He,*
> *Which we cannot comprehend.*

Since He controls the elements, does not God also govern man?

Chap. 37:7
> *He sealeth up the hand of every man;*
> *That all men may know His work.*

The storm intensifies; the wind becomes raw. Bitter ice and hail fall on the land, and now a blizzard rages. Does God send the storm to correct the land? Or will the storm provide moisture for summer wheat?

Chap. 37:12,13
> *And it is turned round about by His*
>   *counsels:*
> *That they may do whatsoever He*
>   *commandeth them*
> *Upon the face of the world in the earth.*
> *He causeth it to come,*
>   *Whether for correction,*
>   *Or for His land, Or for mercy.*

The workings of God are so mysterious, so unfathomable, that no man can duplicate them.

Chap. 37:16,18
> *Dost thou know the balancings of*
>   *the clouds,*
> *The wondrous works of Him which is*
>   *perfect in knowledge?*

Hast thou with Him spread out the sky,
Which is strong, and as a molten
looking glass?

Elihu's paean ends with the emphasis on God's eternal, omnipotent nature:

Touching the Almighty,   Chap. 37:23
We cannot find Him out:
  He is excellent in power,
And in judgment, And in plenty of justice:
  He will not afflict.

Elihu has emphasized God's infinite concern and compassion for His creation. He has stressed that there is a divine plan that includes man and the universe.

If man does not find himself the recipient of good, he must reconcile himself to God and to His plan, not expecting the omnipotent Being to reconcile Himself to man. God is *not* the author of evil.

Infinite Mind, God, speaks to man in various ways and protects him from evil; but man worships on the wrong premise if he serves God for material gain. Gratitude is an important asset in worshipping God, and to extol and magnify Him is the highest and holiest work of man. It is God's infinite power that governs man and the universe.

Elihu's intense convictions and love for God succeed in raising Job's thought to the contemplation of the Allness of God.

In this exalted state Job forgets himself. Lost in the greatness and glory of God, Job hears God speak from the center of the storm.

VII   Arise, Job!

The poet-dramatist makes The Voice an external manifestation, since, in drama, the thought and motive must be audible and visible.

In a theophany, or visible manifestation of God, the mystical experience is personal and often indiscernible to others. It is a "still, small voice" of inner consciousness that mirrors and reveals God to man.

The Voice speaks to Job from within. In this awareness of awakened vision, Job ponders with awe the majesty of the Creator.

Chap. 38:2   During his resentment, it is pointed out that Job "darkeneth counsel by words without knowledge."

Chap. 38:4   The Voice asks, "Where wast thou when I laid the foundations of the earth?"

Chap. 38:7
> *When the morning stars sang together,*
> *And all the sons of God shouted for*
> *joy?*

Chap. 38:4   All the glories of an eternal, unfolding
to 39:30   cosmos expand like ripples and waves in Job's thought, with himself at the center. He considers the breadth and stability of the earth, the depth and boundlessness of the seas, the awakening of the morning, and the vastness of the night. Only an infinite, eternal Deity could perpetuate the ever-changing, panorama of the universe.!

In a breathless moment of self-knowledge, Job recognizes man's coexistence with God:

> *Knowest thou it, because thou wast*   Chap. 38:21
>   *then born?*
> *Or because the number of thy days is*
>   *great?*

In other words:

> *Knowest I it, because I was then born?*
> *Or because the number of my days is*
>   *great?*

Being a dweller-under-the-sky, Job had reveled
in the beauties and gorgeousness of nature.
The storm stimulates him to contemplate the
very source of the snow and hail:

> *By what way is the light parted,*   Chap. 38:24-28a
> *Which scattereth the east wind upon*
>   *the earth?*
> *Who hath divided a watercourse for*
>   *the overflowing of waters,*
> *Or a way for the lightning of thunder;*
>   *To cause it to rain on the earth,*
>   *Where no man is;*
>   *On the wilderness,*
>   *Wherein there is no man;*
> *To satisfy the desolate and waste*
>   *ground;*
> *And to cause the bud of the tender*
>   *herb to spring forth?*
> *Hath the rain a father? . . .*

God, in His tender mercy, preserves and
sustains His earth for its own sake, and not for
the profit of man. After meditating upon the

splendors of the earth, Job's thought embraces
the universe, and he asks these questions of
himself:

Chap. 38:31-33
> *Canst thou bind the sweet influences*
> *of Pleiades,*
> *Or loose the bands of Orion?*
> *Canst thou bring forth Mazzaroth in*
> *his season?*
> *Or canst thou guide Arcturus with his*
> *sons?*
> *Knowest thou the ordinances of*
> *heaven?*
> *Canst thou set the dominion thereof in*
> *the earth?*

Suddenly, he has a flash of insight that answers
his question, "Where can wisdom be found?" It
is in God:

Chap. 38:36
> *Who hath put wisdom in the inward*
> *parts.*
> *Or who hath given understanding to*
> *the heart.*

Man may search the world and the
universe for wisdom, exhausting himself in his
quest, yet never dreaming that it has been
successfully concealed right on his own premises.

Job's consideration turns next to the needs of
the wild animals. Who cares for them? He has
perhaps never given their necessities a passing
thought; now, in open reverence, he
recognizes that the Creator provides for the
needs of the untamed creatures:

Wilt thou hunt the prey for the lion?	Chap. 38:39
Or fill the appetite of the young lions,	

Who provideth for the raven his food?	Chap. 38:41
When his young ones cry unto God,	
They wander for lack of meat.	

Knowest thou the time when the wild goats	Chap. 39:1
Of the rock bring forth?	
Or canst thou mark when the hinds do calve?	

Who hath sent out the wild ass free?	Chap. 39:5
Or who hath loosed the bands of the wild ass?	

Will the unicorn be willing to serve thee?	Chap. 39:9a

Has thou given the horse strength?	Chap. 39:19
Hast thou clothed his neck with thunder?	

Job looks up to see the circling hawk and the soaring eagle:

Doth the hawk fly by thy wisdom,	Chap. 39:26,27
And stretch her wings toward the south?	
Doth the eagle mount up at thy command,	
And make her nest on high?	

When he recognizes that God cares for everything in His universe, he rejoices in the knowledge that God cares for him also!

In this moment of supreme happiness, God's divine love fills Job's consciousness. With his mind so full of the majesty of God, he conjectures how small and insignificant he is in the scheme of the infinite:

Chap. 40:4

Behold, I am vile;
What shall I answer Thee?
I will lay mine hand upon my mouth.

Chap. 40:5

Once have I spoken;
But I will not answer:
Yea, twice;
But I will proceed no further.

But this is not the final disclosure to Job. It is not to God's glory that His manifestation should belittle itself. Will Job disavow God's judgment? Job hears the command:

Chap. 40:10

Deck thyself now with majesty and
excellency;
And array thyself with glory and
beauty .

Job must bring himself into relation with the divine, and change his level of perception from that of a lowly worm, which is material, to that of a spiritual being. Having reached that point of development, Job will no longer need a mediator or intercessor, because:

Chap. 40:14

Then will I also confess unto thee
That thine own right hand can save
thee.

As Job reflects upon this revelation, he questions the source of his strength. The two strongest and most invincible animals come to Job's attention: the behemoth and the leviathan. From whom do *they* receive their strength, if it isn't God? Job acknowledges:

> *I know that Thou canst do every thing,*   Chap. 42:2
> *And that no thought can be*
>   *withholden from thee.*

In candid introspection, Job recognizes that he has been guilty—not of ethical or moral crimes—but of distrust in the goodness and allness of God:

> *Therefore have I uttered that I*   Chap. 42:3bc
>   *understood not;*
> *Things too wonderful for me, which I*
>   *knew not.*

It is to God that Job must look for survival and security:

> *I will demand of Thee, and declare*   Chap. 42:4b
>   *Thou unto ME.*

In joyous recognition, Job cries that he has heard of the Almighty through tradition, but at last the veil has been removed:

> *I have heard of Thee by the hearing of*   Chap. 42:5
>   *the ear:*
> *But now mine eye seeth Thee.*

Finally, he knows that the Omnipotent One cares for every living thing, even himself; and Job repents of his self-centered thinking:

> *Wherefore I abhor myself,*   Chap. 42:6
> *And repent in dust and ashes.*

VIII Triumphant Job

Although the poet-dramatist does not return to the court of the Lord, the implication is clear. Satan loses his bid for supremacy; never again can evil claim to be as powerful as good. Job has withstood the test.

But Satan does not stop trying. There is still one place where Job might be tripped up. Although he cannot resent God, Job might resent his former friends.

Certainly it has been proven that Job's questions and doubts are more acceptable to God than the self-righteousness of Job's companions, who assumed that they were right.

Chap. 42:7,8 The three patiarchs find themselves the object of God's wrath, and only Job's forgiveness can save them. Job's rectitude wins his own freedom and that of his companions. He has no resentment toward his friends. He knows they tried to help him find the cause of his suffering, misguided though they were. Chap. 42:10

Job's financial recovery is not the result of a supernatural deed, but the application of his own business acumen, bestowed upon him by the Creator. When his physical deformities disappear, so that he is no longer ostracized by society, then come "all his brethren, and all his sisters, and all they that had been of his acquaintance before." Chap. 42:11a

Along with their sympathy, "every man also gave him a piece of money, and every one an earring of gold." Each piece of money is enough to buy a small ewe. The ring of gold is collateral. Chap. 42:11c

Job's dearest wish is realized. He has sons and daughters who love and worship God, even as their father does, and both daughters and sons share in their father's rich inheritance. The author does not tell us whether these children are those of a later marriage, or if the earlier report of his children's death was just a horrible mistake. Chap. 42:15

The point is made that "the Lord blessed the latter end of Job more than his beginning." Job's integrity has redeemed him. Chap. 42:12

In his suffering and triumph, Job found pardon and became an example for the world. Storytellers repeated his victory around campfires, and later an unknown poet-dramatist put his triumph into a book to be read by all future generations.

Job may not have known the reason for his trial, but he proved that with every acknowledgement of God's omnipotence, Satan's bid for power is diminished.

The End